The Birthday

Story by Debbie Croft
Illustrations by Debbie Mourtzios

On Saturday morning,
Mum said to Tess and Danny,
"We are all going
to a birthday party."

"Oh, good!" said Tess.
"I love birthday parties!"

"Who is the party for?" said Danny.

"It's for a little boy who is one today," said Mum.

"We will have to buy him a present before we go," said Tess.

"Look!" said Mum with a smile.
"His present is in this box."

"Bananas and apples!" said Tess.
"That's not a good present!"

"Let's get him a car," said Danny.
"Little boys like playing with cars!"

"This birthday boy likes bananas and apples," said Mum.
"Come on. It's time to go."

Tess looked at Danny.
"I **don't** want to go to this party," she said.

Mum stopped the car at the zoo. "The party is in here," she said.

Tess and Danny walked very slowly to the gate.

"The presents go here in this big box," said a man at the gate. "The party is down at the pool. The birthday boy is there with his mother."

Tess and Danny and Mum walked down the long path to the pool.

"Look, Tess!" said Danny.

"I can see the birthday boy.

He's a baby elephant!"

"He can't play with a car," laughed Tess.

"But he can **eat** our present."